ELEMENTARY

the Language of Song

Selected and edited by Nicola-Jane Kemp
and Heidi Pegler

FABER *ff* MUSIC

CONTENTS

HOW TO USE THIS BOOK

The Language of Song series was devised especially for the student singer as an introduction to a wealth of classical song repertoire, and to give them the tools and confidence required to sing in the primary mainland European languages. For this reason, no sung English translations are provided. The songs have been carefully chosen for their appropriateness of text and vocal range for the young student singer.

Preface to each song

Each song or aria is prefaced by a page of notes, containing: a brief background (setting it in its historical context or, where appropriate, its place in the drama); an idiomatic translation; and a phonetic pronunciation of the text. Any further notes at the bottom of each page highlight particular language points that may arise in the individual texts.

Translations: There are two translations for each song or aria. The first is a word-for-word translation directly underneath the text in the musical score. This is to enable the student to see exactly which words will be important for emphasis and interpretation. In addition, the prefatory page to each song includes an idiomatic translation, which will clarify the meaning of the text in grammatical English.

Phonetic pronunciation: A phonetic pronunciation of the original language, using the International Phonetic Alphabet (IPA), is provided for each song. A key to pronunciation is provided for each language at the back of this book and includes both examples from the song texts together with the closest English equivalents to the sounds explained. IPA symbols are given in these guides and careful study of these pages will be required in order to fully understand the IPA symbols that accompany the text for each song or aria. These are some of the basic principles that will help the singer to work along the right lines until they are able to refine pronunciation further with the help of a specialist language coach.

The accompanying CD

The CD provides the text for each song or aria spoken by the language consultants, all of whom are native speakers and work regularly with professional singers (see Biographies on pages 3 and 4). The speakers have attempted to make the text as clear as possible whilst maintaining the overall flow and dramatic content of the language. It is recommended that the language texts are prepared independently from the musical melody at first, as follows:

- Read the pronunciation key for the relevant language.
- Listen to the text on the CD, following the IPA guide for the song.
- Practise speaking the text slowly and clearly.
- When confident, slowly speak the text in the rhythm of the music.
- Gradually increase your speed to match the speed of the song.
- Additionally, practise delivering the text as a dramatic recitation showing your understanding of the language.

The CD also includes backing accompaniments for each song or aria. It should be remembered that these are a practice aid only and should not be substituted for a live accompaniment in performance.

Wherever possible, every effort has been made to return to the original source material. New accompaniments have been arranged for the Arie Antique and some (optional) ornamentation suggested, which appears in small staff notation above the vocal line. Editorial additions, such as dynamics, appear in square brackets.

EDITORS/CONSULTANTS: BIOGRAPHIES

Nicola-Jane Kemp

Nicola-Jane is an examiner for the Associated Board of the Royal Schools of Music and teaches voice to choral scholars at Clare College, Cambridge and St Paul's Girls' School, Hammersmith, London. She is also a professional singer, specialising in the coloratura repertoire (her signature role is 'Queen of the Night'), and works for companies as diverse as Music Theatre Wales and the Festival d'Aix-en-Provence, France. She has been broadcast on BBC Radio and her concert work takes her all round the UK – including the South Bank, Barbican, St Martin-in-the-Fields and St John's Smith Square in London – and to the Middle East.

Heidi Pegler

Heidi is Head of Singing at St Paul's Girls' School, where she runs a lively and busy singing department. She is an examiner for the Associated Board of the Royal Schools of Music and was a contributor on both *A Common Approach 2002* and *All Together!* – a book focusing on teaching music in groups (ABRSM). As a professional singer, she specialises in Baroque music (her debut solo CD, *Hark! The echoing air*, features Baroque music for Soprano, Trumpet and Orchestra) and has performed at many of Britain's leading venues including the Royal Albert Hall, Liverpool Philharmonic Hall, Bridgewater Hall, St David's Hall and the Royal Concert Hall, Glasgow.

Tina Ruta (Italian Consultant)

Born in Naples, Tina studied there at the Conservatoire San Pietro a Maiella and continued with Mark Raphael and Herbert-Caesari in England. She has sung in opera and recitals in England, France and Italy, and performed in West End theatre and at Glyndebourne. She has since gone on to develop a highly sought-after practice as an Italian language coach and has taught at the Guildhall School of Music and Drama and Trinity College of Music, both of which awarded her fellowships. She has coached singers for all the major European opera houses (including Covent Garden, Le Châtelet, Opera-Bastille, Berlin State Opera and Vienna State Opera) and has collaborated with many conductors including Giulini, Muti, Sinopoli, Colin Davis, Myung Whun Chung and Pappano. She also translates film scripts, librettos and lyrics.

Franziska Roth (German Consultant)

Franziska was born and grew up in Germany. She studied musicology at Salzburg University and continued her studies in piano and singing at the 'Mozarteum' Academy of Music. She has worked as a language coach for opera productions at Covent Garden, Glyndebourne, Le Châtelet and Opera-Bastille in Paris; festivals in Aix-en-Provence and Salzburg; and for staged projects in the Carnegie Hall, New York. She is highly sought after by many of the world's leading singers as a Lieder and oratorio coach, and has worked for many great conductors including Barenboim, Rattle, Solti, Haitink, Ghergiev, Pappano, Gardiner and Theilemann. She has been a member of the teaching staff at the Royal College of Music, London since 1989.

Michel Vallat (French Consultant)

Michel Vallat was born in France. He studied at the Sorbonne in Paris, where he graduated with a degree in Philosophy and at the Conservatoire National Superieur de Musique de Paris, where he won both the *Premier Prix de chant* and the *Premier Prix d'Art lyrique*. He was appointed as a French coach at the Royal College of Music and as a Professor of Singing at the Guildhall School of Music and Drama, London. Michel works regularly with the Welsh National Opera, the Scottish Opera, the Glyndebourne Festival and the Royal Opera House (Covent Garden), and with singers such as Valerie Masterson, Della Jones, Thomas Hampson, Sergei Leiferkus, Bruce Ford, Renée Fleming, David Daniels, Sally Matthews, Joseph Calleja, Angelika Kirchschlager and Christopher Maltman.

© 2009 by Faber Music Ltd
First published in 2006 by Faber Music Ltd
This corrected edition first published in 2009
Bloomsbury House 74–77 Great Russell Street London WC1B 3DA
Cover design by Økvik Design
Music processed by MusicSet 2000
Printed in England by Caligraving Ltd
All rights reserved

ISBN10: 0-571-52346-3
EAN13: 978-0-571-53246-7

To buy Faber Music publications or to find out about the full range of titles available
please contact your local music retailer or Faber Music sales enquiries:

Faber Music Limited, Burnt Mill, Elizabeth Way, Harlow, CM20 2HX England
Tel: +44 (0)1279 82 89 82   Fax: +44 (0)1279 82 89 83
sales@fabermusic.com   fabermusic.com

CD recorded in Rectory Studio, High Wycombe, August 2005–May 2006
Piano: John Lenehan; Language consultants: Tina Ruta, Franziska Roth, Michel Vallat
Recorded by John Lenehan; Produced by Nicola-Jane Kemp & Heidi Pegler
℗ 2006 Faber Music Ltd © 2006 Faber Music Ltd

Caro mio ben

My dear beloved   **Tommaso Giordani (1730–1806)**

Background

Born in Naples, Tommaso Giordani lived his life in Dublin and London. Not only was he a prolific composer, writing many overtures, sonatas, concertos and some operas, he was also famed for the many concerts he organised. It is believed that *Caro mio ben*, now a staple song in the student singer's repertoire, was composed for one of these events. There is some dispute as to whether this was composed by Tommaso or Giuseppe Giordani (1743–98).

Idiomatic translation

My dear beloved,
believe me at least,
without you,
my heart languishes.

Your faithful one
always sighs.
Cruel one,
cease so much rigidity.

Pronunciation – **Caro mio ben** [kaɾɔ miɔ bɛn]

Caro mio ben,
kaɾɔ miɔ bɛn

credimi almen,
kɾedimialmɛn

senza di te
sɛntsa di te

languisce il cor.
langwiʃeil kɔr

Il tuo fedel
il tuɔ fɛdel

sospira ognor.
sospiraoɲor

Cessa, crudel,
tʃɛs:sa krudel

tanto rigor!
tantɔ rigor

Further notes

This song uses all the Italian vowels in a few words. Remember, the vowels are pure (no diphthongs), even if liaised (i.e. credimi almen). Do be careful to avoid the English 'ng' sound in the word **languisce**. It is an Italian 'n' with the tip of the tongue just behind the upper front teeth.

1 *spoken text*
2 *piano accompaniment*

Caro mio ben

My dear beloved

Poet unknown

Tommaso Giordani
(1730–1806)

Ca - ro mio ben, cre - di - mi al - men, sen - za di
Dear my beloved, believe-me at-least, without [of]

te lan - gui - sce il cor.___ Ca - ro mio ben, sen - za di
you languishes the heart. Dear my beloved, without [of]

Santa Lucia

Saint Lucy   **Teodoro Cottrau (1827–79)**

Background

Santa Lucia is arguably the best-loved of all the songs from Naples (known as the 'city of song'). This Neopolitan song depicts a local romantic spot in the Bay of Naples known as Santa Lucia, a well-known place for lovers to meet, and the lover is encouraging his beloved to join him there. The tune was composed by Teodoro Cottrau, who was a lawyer and publisher. An acquaintance of Verdi, Bellini, Donizetti and Puccini, he composed over fifty tunes, including *Santa Lucia, Addio mia bella Napoli* and *Sorrentina*.

Idiomatic translation

The silver star shines above the sea,
The waves are calm, the wind is fair;
Come to my agile little boat!
Saint Lucy! Saint Lucy!

Pronunciation – **Santa Lucia** [santa lutʃia]

Sul mare luccica l'astro d'argento,

sul mare lut:ʃika lastrɔ dardʒentɔ

Placida è l'onda, prospero è il vento;

platʃidae londa   prɔsperoeil   vɛntɔ

Venite all'agile barchetta mia!

veniteal:ladʒile barket:ta mia

Santa Lucia, Santa Lucia!

santa lutʃia   santa lutʃia

Further notes

All the Italian vowels are used here. The three syllables 'prospero **e** il' (bar 13) need to be sung on one note and a quick liaison is needed to get through them all quickly but clearly, making a stress on the word '**il**'. No glottal stops should be audible at this point.

3 *spoken text*
4 *piano accompaniment*

Santa Lucia

Saint Lucy

Italian folksong

Teodoro Cottrau
(1827–79)

Non lo dirò col labbro

I will not say this with my lips   Georg Frideric Handel (1685–1759)

Background

Handel's opera *Tolomeo* ('Ptolemy') opened at the King's Theatre in Haymarket, London in 1728. Set in ancient Cyprus, the banished joint ruler of Egypt, Ptolemy IX, lives on the island as a shepherd under the name Osmin, while his wife Seleuce takes the name Delia. The king of Cyprus, the despotic Araspe, pursues Seleuce while his sister, Elisa, is in love with Ptolemy. After various twists of the plot, Ptolemy is returned to the throne by his younger brother Alessandro (a castrato role) and is re-united with Seleuce. *Tolomeo* was the last opera written by Handel for the rival sopranos Faustina Bordoni and Francesca Cuzzoni, with the role of Ptolemy taken by the well-known castrato Senesino and the brother – Alessandro – sung by Antonio Baldi. This cavatina is sung in Act I by Alessandro but is more familiar to English audiences as 'Silent Worship', with alternative words by Arthur Somervell.

Idiomatic translation

I will not say this with my lips as they do not have courage;
Maybe the sparks from my eager eyes will reveal the passion I have for you.
My gaze will do the speaking.

Pronunciation – Non lo dirò col labbro [nɔn lo dir̞ɔ kɔl l̞ab:brɔ]

Non lo dirò col labbro che tanto ardir non ha.

nɔn lo dir̞ɔ kɔl l̞ab:brɔ ke t̞antoardir̞   nɔn a

Forse con le faville dell' avide pupille

f̞ɔrse kɔn le favil̞:le del̞:l̞avide pupil̞:le

per dir come tutto ardo lo sguardo parlerà.

·per dir kɔme t̞ut:toard̞ɔ lo zgwar̞dɔ parler̞a

Further notes

Although liaisons are not marked between **tanto ardir**, **dell' avide** and **tutto ardo**, these words are joined together when sung and no separation should be audible between them.

Non lo dirò col labbro

I will not say this with my lips

Nicola Francesco Haym
(1679–1730)

Georg Frideric Handel
(1685–1759)

5 spoken text

6 piano accompaniment

Non lo di-rò col lab-bro che tan-to ar-dir non ha, non lo di-rò col lab-bro, non lo di-rò col lab-bro che tan-to ar-dir non ha, che

Not it I–shall–say with–the lips which such daring not have, not it I–shall–say with–the lips, not it I–shall–say with–the lips which such daring not have, which

14

Sebben, crudele

Though, cruel one   Antonio Caldara (*c.*1670–1736)

Background

Caldara was born in Venice and, as the son of a local violinist, became a choirboy at St Mark's Basilica where Giovanni Legrenzi was Director. A talented musician (he played the viol, cello and keyboard), Caldara was appointed Music Director in 1699 at the court of Prince Ferdinand Carlo Gonzaga, the Duke of Mantua. The Duke was known for squandering money on a lavish lifestyle, which included mounting grand operas. Following the Duke's financial ruin in 1707, Caldara became Music Director for the aristocratic Ruspoli family in Rome, where he wrote the opera *La costanza in amor vince l'inganno* ('Fidelity in love triumphs over treachery') in 1710. This aria (originally for tenor) is taken from the opera and is sung by Aminta, a shepherd, who cannot understand why the shepherdess, Silvia, no longer responds to his love as she once did.

Idiomatic translation

Though you make me languish, cruel one
I will always be true to you and love you.
In the end, I will wear down your pride
by persistently serving you.

Pronunciation– Sebben, crudele [seb:bɛn krudele]

Sebben, crudele, mi fai languir,
seb:bɛn krudele mi fai langwir

sempre fedele ti voglio amar.
sɛmpre fedele ti voʎoamar

Con la lunghezza del mio servir
Kɔn la lunget:tsa del miɔ servir

la tua fierezza saprò stancar.
la tua fjerɛt:tsa saprɔ stankar

Further notes

There are several words in this aria with double consonants (se**bb**en, lun**gh**ezza, fie**re**zza) that need to be emphasised. Once again (as in *Caro mio ben*), do be careful to avoid any 'ng' sound in the word **languir** or **stancar**.

Sebben, crudele

Though, cruel one

Poet unknown

Antonio Caldara
(*c*.1670–1736)

7 spoken text
8 piano accompaniment

Original key
E minor

Allegretto [♩ = *c*.112]

[*mf*]

Seb - ben, cru - de - le,___ mi fai lan - guir,___
Though, cruel-one, me you-make languish,

Seb - ben,___ cru - de - le,___ mi fai lan -
Though, cruel-one, me you-make languish,

- guir,___ sem - pre fe - de - le, sem - pre fe - de - le___ ti
always faithful, always faithful you

[*mp*]

Nina

Nina   **Anonymous (18th century)**

Background

First performed in London in 1749, this song was included in the opera *Gli tre cicisbei ridicoli* ('The Three Silly Suitors'), although no character called Nina actually exists in the plot. The opera comprised songs by a variety of composers but it was the song 'Nina' that became most popular. Several possible composers have been suggested as the song's authors but no proven sources are available for any of them.

Idiomatic translation

VERSE 1
Nina has stayed in her bed for three days.
This sleep is killing her. For pity's sake, wake her up!
Cymbals, drums, pipes – wake up my Ninetta,
so that she won't slumber any more.

VERSE 2
And while the doctor goes to visit her,
love-sick Nina, stays in bed.
Drums, pipes, cymbals – wake up my Ninetta,
so that she won't slumber any more.

Pronunciation – **Nina** [N<u>i</u>na]

VERSE 1

Tre giorni son che Nina
tre ʤorni sɔn ke N<u>i</u>na

In letto se ne sta.
in l<u>e</u>t:to se ne sta

Il sonno l'assassina,
il s<u>o</u>n:no las:sas:s<u>i</u>na

Svegliatela per pietà!
zveʎ<u>a</u>t<u>e</u>la pɛr pjet<u>a</u>

E cimbali‿e timpani‿e pifferi,
e tʃimbali<u>e</u> timpani<u>e</u> p<u>i</u>f:fɛri

svegliatemi Ninetta,
zveʎ<u>a</u>temi nin<u>e</u>t:ta

perché non dorma più.
pɛrk<u>e</u> nɔn d<u>o</u>rma pj<u>u</u>

VERSE 2

E mentre‿il sior dottore
e m<u>e</u>ntreil sjor dɔt:t<u>o</u>re

A visitarla va,
a vizit<u>a</u>rla va

Ninetta per amore,
nin<u>e</u>t:ta pɛr am<u>o</u>re

In letto se ne sta.
in l<u>e</u>t:to se ne sta

E timpani‿e pifferi‿e cimbali,
e t<u>i</u>mpani<u>e</u> p<u>i</u>f:fɛri<u>e</u> tʃimbali

svegliatemi Ninetta,
zveʎ<u>a</u>temi nin<u>e</u>t:ta

perché non dorma più.
pɛrk<u>e</u> nɔn d<u>o</u>rma pj<u>u</u>

Further notes

In the refrain, the word-ends of **cimbali** and **timpani** are joined to the **e** as if one word (see guide above).

Nina

Nina

Poet unknown

Anonymous (18th century)

Andantino [♩ = c.80]

Original key
G minor

[mf]

[mp]

[mf]

[mf]

Tre gior-ni son che Ni-na, che Ni-na In
Three days are that Nina, that Nina, in

men-tre il sior dot-to - re, dot-to - re A
while the sir doctor, doctor, to

tr

let - to se ne sta, In let - to se ne
bed [herself from–there] stays, in bed [herself from–there]

vi - si-tar - la va, A vi - si-tar - la
visit–her goes, to visit–her

ché non dor -ma più,___ per - ché__ non__ dor - ma__ più, sve -glia- te - mi Ni -
not she–may–slumber more, so–that not she–may–slumber more, waken–her–[for]–me little–Nina,

-net - ta,___ Ni - net - ta, per - ché__ non dor - ma__ più.
little–Nina, so–that not she–may–slumber more.

E
And

Alma del core

Soul of my heart   **Antonio Caldara (*c.*1670–1736)**

Background

This aria comes from Act I of the 1710 version of the opera *La costanza in amor vince l'inganno* ('Fidelity in love triumphs over treachery'); it had disappeared from the printed libretto, however, when the opera was repeated the following year in Rome. Clizia expresses her love and promises to be faithful to Tirsi who sings a second verse, omitted here, promising to return her fidelity to him. (See *Sebben, crudele* for more background notes.)

Idiomatic translation

Soul of my heart, spirit of my being,
I will adore you faithfully forever.
I will be happy in my torment
if I can kiss those beautiful lips.

Pronunciation – **Alma del core** [ˈalma dɛl ˈkɔre]

Alma del core, spirto dell' alma,

ˈalma dɛl ˈkɔre ˈspirtɔ delːˈlalma

sempre costante t'adorerò!

ˈsɛmpre kɔsˈtante tadoreˈrɔ

Sarò contento nel mio tormento

saˈrɔ kɔnˈtɛntɔ nɛl ˈmiɔ tɔrˈmɛntɔ

se quel bel labbro baciar potrò.

se kwel bɛl ˈlabːbrɔ baˈtʃar poˈtrɔ

Further notes

Observe the difference in pronunciation between the rolled [r] and the flipped [ɾ] where marked. (See *Key to International Phonetic Alphabet for Italian*, page 77.)

Alma del core

Soul of my heart

11 *spoken text*
12 *piano accompaniment*

Poet unknown

Antonio Caldara
(*c*.1670–1736)

Allegretto [♩ = *c*.126]

Original key
A major

Recording cue

Al - ma del co - re, spir - to dell' al - ma,
Soul of-the heart, spirit of-the soul,

Al - ma del co - re, spir - to dell'

Al - ma del co - re, spir - to dell'
Soul of-the heart, spirit of-the

al - ma, sem - pre co - stan - te
al - ma, sem - pre co - stan - te t'a - do - re - rò,
soul, forever faithful you I-will-adore,

t'a - do - re - rò, t'a - do - re - rò,
you I-will-adore, you I-will-adore,

Nel cor più non mi sento

I no longer feel in my heart   Giovanni Paisiello (1740–1816)

Background

'Nel cor più non mi sento' comes from the opera *L'amor contrastato* ('Opposition to love'), also known as *La Bella Molinara* ('The Beautiful Miller-Woman'), and was one of many comic operas written by Paisiello. Paisiello worked at the court of Catherine the Great of Russia but this opera was first performed in Naples in 1789; 'Nel cor' achieved memorable popularity as it occurs several times in the same scene, sung by different characters. Initially it is sung by Rachelina, who is working at her rustic home near Naples. A wealthy mill-owner, she is being pursued by three suitors and is rather confused by the whole business of love. In the opera, the second verse is sung by the tenor Calsandro, with the last section as a duet; in concert performance, however, one singer can legitimately sing both verses.

Idiomatic translation

VERSE 1 (FEMALE)

I no longer feel youthfulness sparkling in my heart.
Love, you are guilty of causing me this torment.

REFRAIN

You tease me, you gnaw away at me,
you sting me, you pinch me.
Alas! What is this thing? Pity! Pity! Pity!
Love is a certain thing which makes me despair.

VERSE 2 (MALE)

I do hear you, yes, I hear you, beautiful flower of youth.
My soul, it is you who are the cause of my torment.

REFRAIN

You tease me, you gnaw away at me,
you sting me, you pinch me.
Alas! What is this thing? Pity! Pity! Pity!
That face has a certain something which makes me delirious.

Pronunciation – Nel cor più non mi sento [nɛl kɔr pju nɔn mi sɛntɔ]

VERSE 1 (FEMALE)

Nel cor più non mi sento brillar la gioventù;
nɛl kɔr pju nɔn mi sɛntɔ bril:lar la dʒoventu

cagion del mio tormento, amor, ci hai colpa tu.
kadʒon dɛl miɔ tɔrmentoamor   tʃiai kolpa tu

REFRAIN

Mi stuzzichi, mi mastichi,
mi stut:siki   mi mastiki

mi pungichi, mi pizzichi;
mi pundʒiki   mi pit:siki

che cosa è questo, ahimè? Pietà, pietà, pietà!
ke kɔsaɛ kwɛstoaime   pjeta pjeta pjeta

Amor' è un certo che, che disperar mi fa!
amorɛun   tʃɛrtɔ ke   ke disperar mi fa

VERSE 2 (MALE)

Ti sento, sì, ti sento, bel fior di gioventù;
ti sɛntɔ si ti sɛntɔ   bɛl fjor di dʒoventu

cagion del mio tormento, anima mia sei tu.
kadʒon dɛl miɔ tɔrmentoanima   mia sei tu

REFRAIN

Mi stuzzichi, mi mastichi,
mi stut:siki   mi mastiki

mi pungichi, mi pizzichi;
mi pundʒiki   mi pit:siki

che cosa è questo, ahimè? Pietà, pietà, pietà!
ke kɔsaɛ kwɛstoaime   pjeta pjeta pjeta

Quel viso ha un certo che, che delirar mi fa!
kwel vizoaun   tʃɛrtɔ ke   ke delirar mi fa

Further notes

The liaisons and word stresses are shown clearly above. Emphasising the double consonants in the refrain will help bring out the humour in this aria.

Nel cor più non mi sento

I no longer feel in my heart

spoken text
piano accompaniment

Giuseppe Palomba
(1769–1825)

Giovanni Paisiello
(1740–1816)

* Recording cue

tà, pie-tà, pie-tà!_____ Quel vi - so ha un cer - to_____

tà, pie-tà, pie-tà!_____ A - mor' è un cer - to
pity, pity! Love is a certain

Quel vi - so ha un cer - to
That face has a certain

che, che de - li - rar mi

che, che dis - per - ar mi fa! 2. Ti
something that to–despair me makes! You

che, che de - li - rar mi
something, that to–frenzy me

fa!
makes!

Vittoria, mio core!

Victory, my heart!   Giacomo Carissimi (1605–74)

Background

Carissimi was a well-known singer and organist in Rome. He trained as a choirboy at Tivoli Cathedral and in 1629 was appointed as director of music at the Jesuit Collegio Germanico in Rome. He was to remain there for the rest of his life, despite other offers (including the opportunity to succeed Monteverdi at St Mark's Basilica in Venice), becoming a Jesuit priest in 1637. Although known primarily for his church music, he wrote around 150 cantatas for private performance in wealthy homes. In *Vittoria, mio core!*, one of the shortest and least complex of these, the singer celebrates the triumph of his freedom from feminine wiles. The song has enjoyed a long popularity, both in Italy and beyond, and represents a fine example of the early *Bel Canto* style.

Idiomatic translation

REFRAIN

Victory, my heart! Weep no longer.
It is released from the vile slavery of love.

VERSE 1

Before, the evil woman damaged you with many
glances and used false charms to deceive.
The lies and agonies have no place any more,
the ardour of her cruel fire is extinguished!

VERSE 2

Her smiling eyes no longer dart
arrows that shoot a mortal wound into my breast.
Pain and torment can no longer weaken me;
every tie is broken, all fear has gone!

Pronunciation – Vittoria, mio core! [vit:tɔrja miɔ kɔre]

REFRAIN

Vittoria, mio core! Non lagrimar più.

vit:tɔrja miɔ kɔre nɔn lagrimar pju

È sciolta d'amore la vil servitù.

ɛ ʃɔlta damore la vil sɛrvitu

VERSE 1

Già l'empia a' tuoi danni, fra stuolo di sguardi,

dʒa lempja twoi dan:ni fra stwolɔ di zgwardi

Con vezzi bugiardi dispose gl'inganni;

kɔn vet:si budʒardi dispoze ʎingan:ni

Le frode, gli affanni non hanno più loco,

le frɔde ʎaf:fan:ni nɔn an:nɔ pju lɔkɔ

Del crudo suo foco è spento l'ardore!

del krudɔ suo fɔkɔ ɛ spɛntɔ lardɔre

VERSE 2

Da luci ridenti non esce più strale

da lutʃi ridɛnti nɔn ɛsʃe pju strale

Che piaga mortale nel petto m'avventi:

ke pjaga mortale nɛl pɛt:tɔ mav:vɛnti

Nel duol, ne' tormenti io più non mi sfaccio;

nɛl dwɔl ne tɔrmɛnti io pju nɔn mi sfat:ʃo

È rotto ogni laccio, sparito il timore!

ɛ rɔt:toɲi lat:ʃo sparitɔil timore

Further notes

The spirit in which the singer energises the word **Vittoria** will really help characterise the text. Do be careful not to expel too much air with any of the t's, even on double consonants.

Vittoria, mio core!

Victory, my heart!

15 spoken text

16 piano accompaniment

Domenico Benigni
(b?–d.1653)

Giacomo Carissimi
(1605–74)

36

Gruß

Greeting   Jakob Ludwig Felix Mendelssohn (1809–47) Op. 19, No. 5

Background

Mendelssohn was born into a Jewish family in Hamburg. He was a gifted musician, composer, pianist and conductor, as well as an artist and poet. He travelled widely throughout Europe, where he was much admired – particularly in Britain. While staying in Scotland, he was inspired to write *Die Hebriden*, Op. 26 (popularly known as 'Fingal's Cave'); and of his oratorios, *Elijah* is perhaps his most well-known. Mendelssohn wrote many charming songs and, although he is not generally considered as important a lieder composer as some of his contemporaries, this setting of a text by Heinrich Heine, with its gentle simplicity, is one of his best-loved songs. The poet is full of happy anticipation of love blossoming in spring and sends a greeting to his beloved as if through the sound of bells.

Idiomatic translation

VERSE 1

A lovely ringing sound softly
flows through my mind.
Sound, little spring-time song,
sound out far and wide

VERSE 2

Flow out until you reach the house
where the violets are in bud.
And if you see a rose,
send her my greeting.

Pronunciation – Gruß [grʊs]

VERSE 1

Leise zieht durch mein Gemüt

laizə tsiːt dʊrç main gəmyːt

liebliches Geläute;

liːplɪçəs gəlɔitə

klinge, kleines Frühlingslied,

klɪŋə klainəs fryːlɪŋsliːt

kling hinaus ins Weite.

klɪŋ hɪnaus |ɪns vaitə

VERSE 2

Zieh' hinaus bis an das Haus,

tsiː hɪnaus bɪs |an das haus

wo die Veilchen sprießen;

vo diː failçən ʃpriːsən

wenn du eine Rose schaust,

ven duː |ainə roːzə ʃaust

sag, ich laß sie grüßen.

zaːk |ɪç las ziː gryːsən

Further notes

Do make sure that the difference between 'u' and 'ü' ('durch' and 'Gemüt', etc.) are pronounced clearly. The diphthongs 'au' and 'ei' give a good opportunity to sing on the open [a] vowel. The word 'durch' can be hard for English speakers to pronounce. Practise saying [dʊr - ɪç], then leave out the [ɪ] – [dʊr - ç], then bring the two sounds closer together.

38

Gruß
Greeting

Heinrich Heine
(1797–1856)

Felix Mendelssohn Op.19 No.5
(1809–47)

Original key
D major

Andante [♩ = *c.*72]

© 2006 by Faber Music Ltd

An die Laute

To the lute

Franz Peter Schubert (1797–1828) D905

Background

This delightful song written in 1827 suggests a lover serenading his beloved, with the piano imitating the plucked strings of a lute. Following its publication, the poet Johann Rochlitz (1796–1842) was inspired to write to Schubert asking him to compose music for another text. However, Rochlitz was so specific about the music and harmonies he wanted to be used (he was also a musician), that Schubert felt he must decline the offer: although he needed the money and was trying to further his reputation, he preferred to select his texts himself and retain his creative autonomy.

Idiomatic translation

VERSE 1

Quieter, quieter, little lute,
whisper what I secretly told you
to that window up there.
Like gentle breezes, moonlight,
and the fragrance of flowers,
waft it to my mistress!

VERSE 2

The neighbour's sons are envious
and in this lovely girl's window
a lonely light still burns.
So be even softer little lute.
Let my chosen one hear you
but not the neighbours!

Pronunciation – An die Laute [ˈan diː lautə]

VERSE 1

Leiser, leiser, kleine Laute,
laizɐ laizɐ klainə lautə

flüstre, was ich dir vertraute,
flʏstrə vas ˈɪç diːɐ fɛɐtrautə

dort zu jenem Fenster hin!
dɔrt tsu jeːnəm fɛnstɐ hɪn

Wie die Wellen sanfter Lüfte,
viː diː vɛlən zanftɐ lʏftə

Mondenglanz und Blumendüfte,
moːndənglants ˈʊnt bluːməndʏftə

send' es der Gebieterin!
zɛnt ˈɛs deːɐ gəbiːtərɪn

VERSE 2

Neidisch sind des Nachbars Söhne,
naidɪʃ zɪnt dɛs naxbaːrs zøːnə

und im Fenster jener Schöne
ˈʊnt ˈɪm fɛnstɐ jeːnɐ ʃøːnə

flimmert noch ein einsam Licht.
flɪmɐt nɔx ˈain ˈainzam lɪçt

Drum noch leiser, kleine Laute:
drʊm nɔx laizɐ klainə lautə

dich vernehme die Vertraute,
dɪç fɛɐneːmə diː fɛɐtrautə

Nachbarn aber, Nachbarn nicht!
naxbaːrn ˈabɐ naxbaːrn nɪçt

Further notes

Practise saying the two different 'ch' sounds, as in 'licht' and 'doch'. Also, be careful to mark the difference between 'u' and 'ü' ('bl<u>u</u>mendüfte'), also [i] as in 'die' and [ɪ] as in 'im', 'licht', 'ich' or 'nicht'.

(19) *spoken text*
(20) *piano accompaniment*

An die Laute
To the lute

Johann Friedrich Rochlitz
(1796–1842)

Franz Schubert D905
(1797–1828)

Kinderwacht

Children's Vigil   Robert Alexander Schumann (1810–56) Op. 79, No. 22

Background

Schumann was born in Zwickau and died in a mental asylum in Bonn aged just 46. He wrote many songs, using texts by some of the great poets of the day, although the author of this particular poem is not known. It comes from the 1849 collection *Liederalbum für die Jugend* ('Song album for the young'): arguably an interesting time to be writing simple children's songs, while revolution raged around him in Europe. Schumann wrote of this cycle, 'I have composed songs for young people, selected only from the best writers, progressing from the easy to the more difficult'. Although it may at first seem a somewhat pious poem, Schumann nevertheless captures a tender humour in the verses through his music.

Idiomatic translation

VERSE 1

When faithful children go to sleep,
two little angels stand by their bed,
cover them up and uncover them,
keeping a loving eye on them.

VERSE 2

But when little children get up in the morning,
both angels go to sleep and
no longer have enough power.
So God himself keeps watch instead.

Pronunciation – Kinderwacht [kɪndɐvaːxt]

VERSE 1

Wenn fromme Kindlein schlafen geh'n
vɛn   frɔmə   kɪntlain   ʃlaːfən   geːn

an ihrem Bettt zwei Englein steh'n,
|an |iːrəm bɛt   tsvai |ɛŋlain   ʃteːn

decken sie zu, decken sie auf,
dɛkən   zi: tsuː dɛkən   zi: |auf

haben ein liebendes Auge drauf.
haːbən |ain liːbəndəs |augə drauf

VERSE 2

Wenn aber auf die Kindlein steh'n,
vɛn |abɐ |auf di: kɪntlain   ʃteːn

die beiden Engel schlafen geh'n,
di: baidən |ɛŋəl ʃlaːfən   geːn

reicht nun nicht mehr der Englein Macht
raiçt   nuːn nıçt   meːɐ deːɐ |ɛŋlain   maxt

der liebe Gott hält selbst die Wacht.
deːɐ liːbə gɔt hɛlt zɛlpst di: vaxt

Further notes

While the melody of this song is relatively simple, the text will need some precise articulation – particularly '**reicht nun nicht mehr der Englein Macht**', which uses both **ch** sounds and is sung with a quicker rhythm.

Kinderwacht

Children's Vigil

Poet unknown

Robert Schumann Op. 79 No. 22
(1810–56)

Einfach *(simply)* [♩ = c.54]

Wenn from-me Kind - lein schla - fen geh'n an
When faithful little–children to–sleep go by

ih - rem Bett zwei Eng - lein steh'n, de - cken sie zu,
their bed two little–angels stand, cover them up,

de - cken sie auf, ha - ben ein lie - ben - des
cover them off, have a loving

Au - ge drauf. Wenn
eye on–them. When

Frühlingslied

Spring Song   Franz Peter Schubert (1797–1828) D398

Background

Schubert set this poem by Ludwig Hölty (originally titled *Mailied* or 'May Song') in 1816, when he was just 19. Finally published posthumously in 1887, the charming text celebrates God's work of creation and the fresh newness of spring, while the accompaniment flows along with its running semiquavers underneath a simple melody. The song's original key of G major is considered a lyrical key associated with love.

Idiomatic translation

VERSE 1

The air is blue, the valley is green,
the lilies of the valley are blooming
and the cowslips, further down.
The meadows, already colourful,
paint themselves daily with more colours.

VERSE 2

So come, those who delight in May,
and look with pleasure at the beautiful world,
and God's fatherly kindness that
produced such splendour,
the tree and its blossom.

Pronunciation – **Frühlingslied** [fryːlɪŋsliːt]

VERSE 1

Die Luft ist blau, das Tal ist grün,

diː lʊft |ɪst blau das taːl |ɪst gryːn

die kleinen Maienglocken blühn,

diː klainən maiənglɔkən blyːn

und Schlüsselblumen drunter;

|ʊnt ʃlysəlbluːmən drʊntɐ

der Wiesengrund ist schon so bunt

deːɐ viːzəngrʊnt |ɪst ʃoːn zoː bʊnt

und malt sich täglich bunter.

|ʊnt malt zɪç teːklɪç bʊntɐ

VERSE 2

Drum komme, wem der Mai gefällt,

drʊm kɔmə veːm deːɐ mai gəfɛlt

und schaue froh die schöne Welt

|ʊnt ʃauə froː diː ʃøːnə vɛlt

und Gottes Vatergüte,

|ʊnt gɔtəs faːtɐgyːtə

die solche Pracht hervorgebracht,

diː zɔlçə praxt hɛɐfoːɐgəbraxt

den Baum und seine Blüte.

deːn baum |ʊnt zainə blyːtə

Further notes

The main language points to note in this text concern the clear differences between the **u** and **ü** vowels throughout, e.g.: 'und Schlüsselblumen drunter' and the **ch** sounds eg: 'die solche Pracht' (see above). The main diphthongs used here are **au** ('blau') and **ai/ei** ('Mai/seine'). As always in this circumstance, the singer needs to maintain the long [a] sound wherever these occur and especially in the high phrase at the end of the song ('Baum').

23 *spoken text*
24 *piano accompaniment*

Frühlingslied
Spring Song

Ludwig H.C. Hölty
(1748–76)

Franz Schubert D398
(1797–1828)

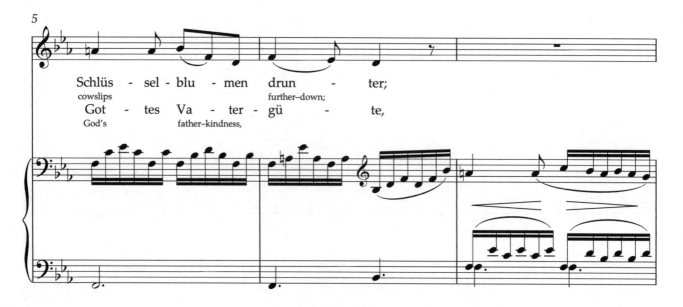

Wiegenlied
Cradle Song
Johannes Brahms (1833–97) Op. 49, No. 4

Background

This well-loved song was originally just one verse long: the second verse, by Georg Scherer (1849), was added later. The last two lines of Scherer's verse were adapted by Brahms when he wrote this song in 1868 for his friends, the Fabers; he remembered Mrs Faber (*née* Bertha Porubsky) singing a lullaby by Alexander Baumann and he cleverly incorporated its melodic figure into the sleep-inducing accompaniment of his song to celebrate the birth of their baby boy. This lovely lullaby forms a prayer for a child, asking guardian angels to protect him from bad dreams and wake again safely in the morning.

Idiomatic translation

VERSE 1
Good evening, good night,
covered by roses and pinks,
slip under the blanket,
and early tomorrow, God-willing,
you will be woken again.

VERSE 2
Good evening, good night,
guarded by little angels,
who show you while you dream,
the Christmas tree.
Now sleep blissfully and sweetly,
and see Paradise in your dreams.

Pronunciation – Wiegenlied [viːgənliːt]

VERSE 1

Guten Abend, gut' Nacht,

guːtən |abənt guːt naxt

mit Rosen bedacht,

mɪt roːzən bədaxt

mit Näg'lein besteckt,

mɪt nɛːglain bəʃtɛkt

schlupf' unter die Deck':

ʃlʊpf |untɐ diː dɛk

Morgen früh, wenn Gott will,

mɔrgən fryː ven gɔt vɪl

wirst du wieder geweckt.

vɪrst duː viːdɐ gəvɛkt

VERSE 2

Guten Abend, gut' Nacht,

guːtən |abənt guːt naxt

von Eng'lein bewacht,

fɔn |ɛŋlain bəvaxt

die zeigen im Traum

diː tsaigən |ɪm traum

dir Christkindleins Baum:

diːɐ krɪstkɪntlains baum

schlaf' nun selig und süß,

ʃlaːf nuːn zeːlɪç |unt zyːs

schau' im Traum's Paradies.

ʃau |ɪm traums paradiːs

Further notes

In the pronunciation of '**Wirst du**', it would be too mannered to pronounce the 't' and 'd' separately. The nearest English equivalent would be in our phrase 'shut down' (i.e. with the 't' joined to the 'd'). The challenge in this song is to make sure that all the consonants are pronounced, yet keeping a legato line. Many words of the first verse end in **-ckt** or **-cht**. These need to be clear and lightly articulated in keeping with the gentle mood of the lullaby.

Wiegenlied
Cradle Song

spoken text
piano accompaniment

German folksong

Johannes Brahms Op. 49 No. 4
(1833–1897)

Zart bewegt *(delicate and moving)* [♩ = c.100]

Gu-ten A - bend, gut' Nacht, mit
Good evening, good night, with

Ro - sen be - dacht, mit Näg'-lein be - steckt, schlupf' un - ter die
roses covered, with pinks stuck–over, slip under the

Deck': Mor-gen früh, wenn Gott will, wirst du wie - der ge -
blanket: Tomorrow early, if God wills, will you again be–awakened,

- weckt, mor-gen früh, wenn Gott will, wirst du wie - der ge - weckt.
tomorrow early, if God wills, will you again be–awakened.

Sonntag

Sunday   Johannes Brahms (1833–97) Op. 47, No. 3

Background

Brahms found and modernised the text for this song from a folksong collection *Alte hoch und niederdeutsche Volkslieder* ('Old high and low German folksongs', published *c*.1845, edited by L. Uhland). The song was composed in around 1860 and first performed in 1871. It is a small masterpiece, which nevertheless displays the common touch in its simple folk-like melody. The young man in this song can hardly contain himself all week, waiting for a glimpse of his sweetheart on Sundays.

Idiomatic translation

VERSE 1

I haven't seen my lovely sweetheart
for an entire week.
I saw her on a Sunday standing in front of the door;
That loveliest young and fair girl,
that loveliest little heart.
God-willing, I would be with her today.

VERSE 2

I haven't stopped laughing
for a whole week.
I saw her go into church on Sunday;
That loveliest young and fair girl, etc.

Pronunciation – Sonntag [zɔntaːk]

VERSE 1

So hab' ich doch die ganze Woche

zoː haːp |ɪç dɔx   diː gantsə vɔxə

mein feines Liebchen nicht geseh'n,

main fainəs liːpçən   nɪçt gəzeːn

ich sah es an einem Sonntag

|ɪç zaː |ɛs |an |ainəm zɔntaːk

wohl vor der Türe steh'n:

voːl foːɐ deːɐ tyːrə ʃteːn

das tausendschöne Jungfräulein,

das tauzəntʃøːnə   yʊŋfrɔilain

das tausendschöne Herzelein,

das tauzəntʃøːnə   hɛrtsəlain

wollte Gott, wollte Gott, ich wär' heute bei ihr!

vɔltə gɔt   vɔltə gɔt |ɪç veːɐ hɔitə bai |iːɐ

VERSE 2

So will mir doch die ganze Woche

zoː vɪl miːɐ dɔx diː gantsə vɔxə

das Lachen nicht vergeh'n,

das laxən   nɪçt fɛɐgeːn

ich sah es an einem Sonntag

|ɪç zaː |ɛs |an |ainəm zɔntaːk

wohl in die Kirche geh'n:

voːl |ɪn diː kɪrçə geːn

Further notes

Because of the speed of this song, much benefit will be gained from speaking the text clearly and slowly at first with all consonants in place before speeding up. The glottal stops will need extra (if gentle) pointing – especially '| ich sah | es | an | einem Sonntag'.

Sonntag
Sunday

27 spoken text
28 piano accompaniment

German folksong

Johannes Brahms Op. 47 No. 3
(1833–97)

Nicht zu langsam (*not too slow*) [♩ = 100–118]

So hab' ich doch die gan- ze Wo- che mein fei- nes
So have I indeed the whole week my lovely

Lieb- chen nicht ge- seh'n, ich sah es an ei- nem Sonn- tag wohl vor der Tü- re
sweet-heart not seen, I saw it (her) on a Sunday right before the door

steh'n: das tau- send- schö- ne Jung- fräu- lein, das tau- send- schö- ne
standing: the thousand-fold-beautiful young-girl, the thousand-fold-beautiful

Her- ze- lein, woll- te Gott, woll- te Gott, ich wär' heu- te bei ihr,
little-heart, (if) willing God, (if) willing God, I were today with her,

woll- te Gott, woll- te Gott, ich wär' heu - te bei ihr!
(if) willing God, (if) willing God, I were today with her!

So will mir
So will to—me

doch die gan-ze Wo-che das__ La - chen nicht ver-geh'n, ich sah
indeed the whole week the laughter not fade, I saw

es an ei-nem Sonn-tag wohl in die Kir-che geh'n: das
it (her) on a Sunday right into the church go: the

36

[*mf*]

tau - send-schö-ne Jung - fräu - lein, das tau - send-schö-ne Her - ze - lein,
thousand–fold–beautiful young–girl, the thousand–fold–beautiful little–heart,

mf

40 [*f*]

woll-te Gott, woll-te Gott, ich wär' heu - te bei ihr,
(if) willing God, (if) willing God, I were today with her,

44 [*p*]

woll-te Gott, woll-te Gott, ich wär' heu - te bei ihr!
(if) willing God, (if) willing God, I were today with her!

p

49

Heidenröslein

Little heathland rose   Franz Peter Schubert (1797–1828) Op. 3, No. 3 (D257)

Background

Written in 1815 and published in 1821, this setting of a poem by Johann Wolfgang von Goethe (1749–1832) comes straight out of the German folksong tradition (one can trace a German folksong about a wild rose back to the sixteenth century). The poem depicts a young boy who picks a wild rose growing on the heath, in spite of her protests. Although he is pricked by her thorns, she can do nothing to stop him. The underlying connotations suggest that this has more to do with boys and girls than boys and wild roses!

Idiomatic translation

VERSE 1

A boy saw a little rose growing on the heath,
as young and lovely as the morning. Quickly, he ran
to see it close up and looked at it with great delight.
Little rose, little red rose, little rose on the heath.

VERSE 2

The boy said, 'I'll pluck you little rose on the heath'.
The little rose said, 'I'll prick you so that you will always
think of me – for I will not endure it.'
Little rose … *etc.*

VERSE 3

But the wild boy plucked the little rose on the heath.
The little rose defended herself and pricked him. But her
cries of pain were to no avail and she simply had to endure it.
Little rose … *etc.*

Pronunciation – Heidenröslein [haɪdənrøːslaɪn]

VERSE 1

Sah ein Knab' ein Röslein stehn,
zaː |aɪn knaːp |aɪn røːslaɪn ʃteːn

war so jung und morgenschön,
vaːr zoː jʊŋ |ʊnt mɔrgənʃøːn

sah's mit vielen Freuden.
zaːs mɪt fiːlən frɔɪdən

Röslein, Röslein, Röslein rot,
røːslaɪn røːslaɪn røːslaɪn roːt

Röslein auf der Heiden,
røːslaɪn |auf deːɐ haɪdən

lief er schnell, es nah zu sehn,
liːf |eːɐ ʃnɛl |ɛs naː tsuː zeːn

Röslein auf der Heiden.
røːslaɪn |auf deːɐ haɪdən

VERSE 2

Knabe sprach: ich breche dich,
knaːbə ʃpraːx |ɪç brɛçə dɪç

Röslein sprach: ich steche dich,
røːslaɪn ʃpraːx |ɪç ʃtɛçə dɪç

und ich will's nicht leiden.
|ʊnt |ɪç vɪls nɪçt laɪdən

Röslein auf der Heiden,
røːslaɪn |auf deːɐ haɪdən

dass du ewig denkst an mich,
das duː |eviç dɛŋkst |an mɪç

VERSE 3

Und der wilde Knabe brach
|ʊnt deːɐ vɪldə knaːbə braːx

Röslein wehrte sich und stach,
røːslaɪn veːrtə zɪç |ʊnt ʃtaːx

mußt es eben leiden.
mʊst |ɛs |eːbən laɪdən

's Röslein auf der Heiden;
srøːslaɪn |auf deːɐ haɪdən

half ihm doch kein Weh und Ach,
half |iːm dɔx kaɪn veː |ʊnt |ax

Further notes

There are many examples of words ending in **-ch** here, so do check the pronunciation guide carefully. Also note the long [i] vowel in the word 'ihm', as opposed to the short [ɪ] in '**nicht**' and '**ich**', etc. Although always necessary, this song particularly benefits from reciting the poem dramatically in German first to get the feel of telling the story clearly.

spoken text
piano accompaniment

Heidenröslein
Little heathland rose

Johann Wolfgang von Goethe
(1749–1832)

Franz Schubert Op. 3 No. 3
(1797–1828)

1. Sah ein Knab' ein Rös-lein stehn, Rös-lein auf der
   Saw a boy a little–rose standing, little–rose on the
2. Kna-be sprach: ich bre-che dich, Rös-lein auf der
   Boy spoke: I pluck you, little–rose on the
3. Und der wil-de Kna-be brach 's Rös-lein auf der
   And the wild boy plucked the little–rose on the

Hei - den, war so jung und mor-gen-schön, lief er schnell, es
heath, (it) was so young and morning–lovely, ran he fast, it
Hei - den! Rös-lein sprach: ich ste-che dich, dass du e-wig
heath! Little–rose spoke: I prick you, so-that you forever
Hei - den; Rös-lein wehr-te sich und stach, half ihm doch kein
heath; Little–rose defended itself and pricked, helped him though no

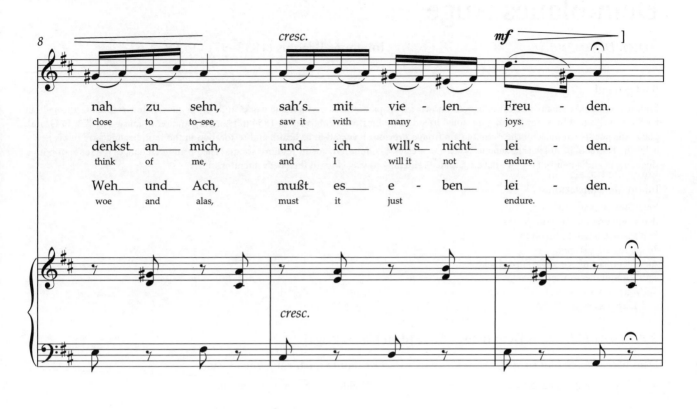

nah___ zu___ sehn, sah's___ mit___ vie - len Freu - den.
close to to–see, saw it with many joys.

denkst an___ mich, und___ ich will's nicht lei - den.
think of me, and I will it not endure.

Weh___ und___ Ach, mußt___ es e - ben lei - den.
woe and alas, must it just endure.

Rös - lein, Rös - lein, Rös - lein___ rot, Rös - lein auf der
Little–rose, little–rose, little–rose red, little–rose on the

Hei - den.
heath.

Dein blaues Auge

Your blue eye   Johannes Brahms (1833–97) Op.59, No. 8

Background

Brahms composed in many genres and is well known for his piano music, symphonic works and choral pieces. He wrote songs throughout his life and this text by Klaus Groth (a personal friend of Brahms) was published in 1854 in Hamburg and set to music in 1873. In Groth's poem, the poet is reminded of the burning pain from a previous love and finds health and restoration in the cool, healing gaze of his new beloved. This cool healing of the wounded heart expresses a common theme in Brahms' songs. (The poem interchanges the sense of both a singular eye and a pair of eyes. We have translated it literally to stay close to the poet's intentions.)

Idiomatic translation

Your blue eye stays so still
that I can look into its very depths.
You ask me, what do I wish to see in it?
To see myself restored.
An ardent pair of eyes once burned me.
That painful memory still smarts.
Yet your eyes are as clear
and as cool as a lake.

Pronunciation – **Dein blaues Auge** [daɪn blaʊəs ˈaʊgə]

Dein blaues Auge hält so still,

daɪn blaʊəs ˈaʊgə hɛlt zoː ʃtɪl

Ich blicke bis zum Grund.

ˈɪç blɪkə bɪs tsʊm grʊnt

Du fragst mich, was ich sehen will?

duː fraːkst mɪç   vas ˈɪç zeːən vɪl

Ich sehe mich gesund.

ˈɪç zeːə mɪç gəzʊnt

Es brannte mich ein glühend Paar,

ˈɛs brantə   mɪç   ˈaɪn glyːənt paːr

Noch schmerzt das Nachgefühl:

nɔx   ʃmɛrtst   das naxgəfyːl

Das deine ist wie See so klar

das daɪnə ˈɪst viː zeː zoː klaːr

Und wie ein See so kühl.

ˈʊnt   viː   ˈaɪn zeː zoː kyːl

Further notes

There are many occasions where glottal stops are required in this song but they should always be subtle and not disturb the line of singing. When you practise speaking the text, work particularly at the consonant clusters (… **fragst mich**, … **schmerzt**, … **Nachgefühl**).

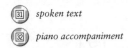

Dein blaues Auge
Your blue eye

Klaus Groth
(1819–99)

Johannes Brahms Op. 59 No. 8
(1833–97)

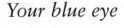

Chevaliers de la table ronde

Knights of the Round Table   **French folksong**

Background

The wine-making regions of Champagne, Bourgogne and Beaujolais are well-known for their local folksongs and choirs: any wine festival in these regions would be incomplete without their local songs performed by the 'Chanteurs de Beaune of the Chevaliers de Tastevin'. This drinking song, or 'Chanson à boire', is from the Bourgogne area of France. There are plenty more rousing verses but we have chosen just three of them.

Idiomatic translation

VERSE 1
Knights of the round table,
Taste and see if the wine is good.
Let's taste and see, yes, yes, yes,
Let's taste and see, no, no, no,
Let's taste and see if the wine is good.

VERSE 2
If it is good, if it is tasty,
I will drink as much of it as I want.
I will drink, … *etc.*

VERSE 3
And if a few drops remain
It will refresh us
It will … *etc.*

Pronunciation – **Chevaliers de la table ronde** [ʃəvalje̱ de la ta̱blə ʀо̱̄də]

VERSE 1

Chevaliers de la table ronde
ʃəvalje̱   de la ta̱blə ʀо̱̄də

Goûtons voir si le vin ǀ est bon.
gu̱tõ   vwaʀ si lə vẽ ɛ bõ

Goûtons voir, oui, oui, oui,
gu̱tõ   vwaʀ wi wi wi

Goûtons voir, non, non, non,
gu̱tõ   vwaʀ nõ nõ nõ

Goûtons voir si le vin ǀ est bon
gu̱tõ   vwaʀ si lə vẽ ɛ bõ

VERSE 2

S'il̯est bon, s'il̯est̯agréable
si(l)ɛ bõ si(l)ɛ(t)agʀe̱a̱blə

J'en boirai jusqu'a mon plaisir.
ʒã bwaʀe̱ ʒy̱ska mõ plɛzi̱ʀ

J'en boirai …
ʒã bwaʀe̱ …

VERSE 3

Et s'il̯en reste quelques gouttes
e si(l)ã ʀe̱stə ke̱lkə   gu̱tə

Ce sera pour nous rafraîchir
sə səʀa̱ puʀ nu   ʀafʀeʃi̱ʀ

Ce sera …
sə səʀa̱ …

Further notes

This lively folksong in typical French style is a fun way to begin singing in French. Do listen closely to the pronunciation guide on the CD and note the liaisons as marked. Be careful not to pronounce any of the **n**'s or **m**'s in the nasal sounds and make the difference between [õ] and [ã] very clear.

Chevaliers de la table ronde
Knights of the Round Table

French folksong (18th century)

spoken text
piano accompaniment

en re-ste quel-ques gout-tes Ce se-ra pour nous ra-fraî-chir. Et s'il
(of –it) remains a–few drops It will for us to–refresh. And if there

- chir. Ce se - ra oui, oui, oui, Ce se - ra non, non, non, Ce se - ra pour nous ra-fraî-
It will yes, yes, yes, It will no, no, no, It will for us to–refresh.

- chir. Ce se - ra oui, oui, oui, Ce se - ra non, non, non, Ce se -
It will yes, yes, yes, It will no, no, no, It will

-ra pour nous ra-fraî-chir.
for us to-refresh.

Bois épais

Deep wood   **Jean-Baptiste Lully (1632–87)**

Background

Born in Italy, Lully was brought to France, as a youth, where he quickly established himself as a flamboyant character – a dancer, comedian and composer. He was appointed to the court of King Louis XIV in 1653 and by 1662 was made Master of Music to the royal household, composing court ballets in which the King often took part. Lully collaborated with Molière on a comic ballet *Le bourgeois gentilhomme* ('The bourgeois gentleman'), thereafter concentrating primarily on composing a style of French opera known as 'tragédies lyriques' (lyric tragedies). His operas, designed to glorify the King, were significant in the development of a distinctive French operatic tradition. His untimely death was due to a gangrenous abscess on his toe, which he accidentally hit during a performance by tapping the floor with his cane, beating time! This *air* comes from one his first operas *Amadis* (1684) with a libretto by Philippe Quinault (1635–88). Amadis is in love with Orianne, but she mistakenly believes him to be unfaithful and has become betrothed to Corisande. At this point, Amadis has entered the forest in the hope that he will find solitude in its shadows. After a convoluted plot involving other characters and magic, the lovers, are of course, united at the end of the opera.

Idiomatic translation

Deep wood, increase your shade;   I feel the extreme horror of despair,
You wouldn't know how to be dark enough,   I must no longer see the object of my love,
You couldn't conceal my unhappy love too much.   I no longer want to endure the light of day.

Pronunciation – **Bois épais** [bwa̲(z)epɛ]

Bois épais redouble ton ombre,   **Je sens un désespoir dont l'horreur est extrême,**

bwa̲(z)epɛ rədu̲blə   tõ(n)õbrə   ʒə sɑ̃(z)œ̃ dezɛspwa̲r dõ   lɔrœ̲(r)ɛ(t)ekstrɛmə

Tu ne saurais être assez sombre,   **Je ne dois plus voir ce que j'aime,**

ty nə so̲rɛ(z)ɛt(r)a̲se   sõ̲brə   ʒə nə dwa ply   vwar sə kə ʒɛmə

Tu ne peux trop cacher   **Je ne veux plus**

ty nə pø   tro kaʃe̲   ʒə nə vø   ply

mon malheureux amour.   **souffrir le jour.**

mõ   malœrœ̲(z)amu̲r   sufri̲r   lə ʒur

Further notes

This beautiful and poignant aria is often sung by young singers, as the French is not too complex. However, do look closely at the liaisons as marked and check that all the different 'e' vowels are understood in their various phonetic sounds. Also the last line is a particular challenge in practising the difference between [u] and [y] as in **plus souffrir le jour**. Although the uvular [r] symbol is used here, it would be considered stylistically appropriate to pronounce rolled r's in the Italian style for French Baroque music (See *Key to International Phonetic Alphabet for French*).

Bois épais
Deep wood

Philippe Quinault
(1635–88)

Jean-Baptiste Lully
(1632–87)

spoken text
piano accompaniment

En prière

In prayer   **Gabriel Urbain Fauré (1845–1924)**

Background

Gabriel Fauré wrote over 100 songs in his lifetime, of which this setting of a poem by Stéphan Bordèse (1847– ?) was composed in 1889 for voice and organ. It was published as part of his second volume of songs by the publishers Hamelle in 1897. Fauré chose his poems with great care, as the words helped dictate the musical patterns. He knew it was very difficult to articulate the text clearly when singing above the stave, so many of his songs are written for a mid-range tessitura – as seen here. *En prière* forms a child-like, perhaps Christ-child's prayer. Its simplicity of faith belies the profound thoughts expressed.

Idiomatic translation

If the voice of a child can ascend to You
Oh my Father,
Listen to Jesus, kneeling before You
in prayer!
If you have chosen me to teach your laws
on earth,
I will know how to serve you, majestic King
of kings, Oh light!
On my lips, Lord, place the saving
truth,

So that he who doubts, with humility,
reveres You!
Do not abandon me, give me the
necessary gentleness
to relieve suffering, to soothe distress
and misery!
Reveal Yourself to me, Lord in whom
I believe and hope:
For You I am willing to suffer and die on the cross
at Calvary.

Pronunciation – En prière [ãn priɛʁə]

Si la voix d'un enfant peut monter jusqu'à Vous,
si la vwa dœ̃(n)ãfã pø mõte ʒyska vu

Ô mon Père,
o mõ pɛʁə

Écoutez de Jésus, devant Vous | à genoux,
ekute də ʒezy dəvã vu a ʒənu

La prière!
la prijɛʁə

Si Vous m'avez choisi pour enseigner vos lois
si vu mave ʃwazi pu(ʁ)ãseɲe vo lwa

Sur la terre,
syʁ la tɛʁə

Je saurai Vous servir, auguste Roi des rois,
ʒə soʁe vu sɛʁviʁ ogystə ʁwa de rwa

Ô Lumière!
o lymjɛʁə

Sur mes lèvres, Seigneur, mettez la vérité
syʁ me lɛvʁə seɲœʁ mete la veʁite

Salutaire,
salytɛʁə

Pour que celui qui doute, avec humilité
puʁ kə səlɥi ki dut avɛ(k)ymilite

Vous révère!
vu ʁevɛʁə

Ne m'abandonnez pas, donnez-moi la douceur
nə mabãdone pa dɔne mwa la dusœʁ

Nécessaire,
nesesɛʁə

Pour apaiser les maux, soulager la douleur,
pu(ʁ)apeze le mo sulaʒe la dulœʁ

La misère!
la mizɛʁə

Révélez Vous à moi, Seigneur en qui je crois
revele vu(z)a mwa seɲœ(ʁ)ã ki ʒə kʁwa

Et j'espère:
e ʒɛspɛʁə

Pour Vous je veux souffrir | et mourir sur la croix,
puʁ vu ʒə vø sufʁiʁ e muʁiʁ syʁ la kʁwa

Au calvaire!
o kalvɛʁə

Further notes

There are some particular challenges for the singer in this song. The text will need some careful preparation aside from the melody. Do give special attention to the difference between [e] and [ɛ] sounds eg: 'révère'; to [u] and [y] sounds eg. 'Écoutez de Jésus, devant Vous à genoux'.

En prière

In prayer

37 *spoken text*

38 *piano accompaniment*

Stéphan Bordèse
(1847– ?)

Gabriel Fauré
(1845–1924)

Si la voix d'un en-fant peut mon-ter jus-qu'à
If the voice of a child can rise as-far as

Vous, Ô mon Pè - re,_____ É - cou - tez de Jé -
You, O my Father, Listen to Jesus,

-sus, de-vant Vous à ge-noux, La pri - è - re!
before You on (his) knees, the prayer!

Si Vous m'a-vez choi - si pour en-sei-gner vos lois Sur la
If You me have chosen in-order to-teach your laws On the

70

Lydia

Lydia · **Gabriel Urbain Fauré (1845–1924) Op. 4 No. 2**

Background

Fauré's musical gifts were recognised as a child, when an elderly blind lady heard him playing the harmonium in the local chapel. He studied at L'École Niedermeyer in Paris, enabling him to mix with other composers and poets of the day, including Saint-Saëns. By the time he was twenty, he had published twenty songs, of which this setting of a poem by Charles-Marie-René Leconte de Lisle (1818–1894) is one. Included in his first collection of 1871, it is thought to have been written around 1870 and is one of his first excursions into the world of the 'exotic'. Lisle was a 'Parnassian' poet – a group who were not interested in romanticism, but reverted to the purity and formality associated with ancient Greek culture. Fauré employs both a musical pun and an 'antique' touch by raising the fourth note of the scale to put the song temporarily into the Lydian mode. *Lydia* was dedicated to Madame Marie Trélat (mezzo soprano) and first performed by her at the Société nationale de musique, 18th May 1872.

Idiomatic translation

VERSE 1

Lydia, on your pink cheeks, and on your neck, so cool and white,
the liquid, gold tresses that you let loose, flow shining down.
This day that shines is best of all; let us forget the eternal grave,
let your kisses, your dove-like kisses, sing on your blossoming lips.

VERSE 2

A hidden lily unceasingly radiates a heavenly scent from within your breast;
innumerable delights emanate from you, young goddess.
I love you and am dying, oh my love; my soul is ravished by your kisses!
O Lydia, return my life to me, that I may die, die (*with love*) over and over again.

Pronunciation – Lydia [li̱dja]

VERSE 1

Lydia sur tes roses joues
li̱dija sуʀ tɛ ʀozə ʒu̯ə

Et sur ton col frais | et si blanc
e sуʀ tõ kɔl fʀɛ   e si blã

Roule étincelant
ʀu(l)etɛ̃səlã

L'or fluide que tu dénoues.
lɔʀ flyi̱də kə ty denu̯ə

Le jour qui luit | est le meilleur,
lə ʒuʀ ki ly̯i   ɛ lə mɛjœʀ

Oublions l'éternelle tombe,
ublijõ̱   letɛʀne̱lə tõ̱bə

Laisse tes baisers de colombe,
lɛsə   tɛ beze̱   də kɔlõ̱bə

Chanter sur ta lèvre en fleur.
ʃã̱te   sуʀ ta le̱v(ʀ)ã   flœ̱ʀ

VERSE 2

Un lys caché répand sans cesse
œ̃ lis kaʃe ʀepã̱   sã   sɛsə

Une odeur divine en ton sein;
y(n)odœʀ divi̱(n)ã tõ sɛ̃

Les délices comme un essaim
lɛ   deli̱sə kɔ(m)œ̃(n)esɛ̱̃

Sortent de toi, jeune déesse.
sɔʀtə   də twa ʒœnə de̱ɛsə

Je t'aime et meurs, ô mes amours,
ʒə tɛ(m)emœ̱ʀ   o mɛ(z)amu̱ʀ

Mon âme en baisers m'est ravie!
mõ(n)a(m)ã beze̱ mɛ ʀavi̱ə

O Lydia, rends-moi la vie,
o li̱dija ʀã   mwa la vi̱ə

Que je puisse mourir, mourir toujours!
kə ʒə py̯isə muʀi̱ʀ muʀi̱ʀ tuʒuʀ

Further notes

Do note the pronunciation of the different 'e' sounds in words such as 'essaim' and 'déesse'. The 's' in 'lys' is sounded.

39 *spoken text*

40 *piano accompaniment*

Lydia
Lydia

Leconte De Lisle
(1818–94)

Gabriel Fauré Op. 4 No. 2
(1845–1924)

© 2006 by Faber Music Ltd

Key to International Phonetic Alphabet for Italian

Vowels	IPA	English sounds		Italian words
A	[a]	as in a bright 'ah'		caro [karɔ]
E	[ɛ]	open as in 'bed'		bella [bɛl:la]
	[e]	closed (prepare your tongue as if to say 'ee' and say 'ay' without dropping the jaw)		che [ke]
I	[i]	as in 'see' or 'police'		mi [mi], ti [ti]
O	[o]	closed (say 'oh' with lips in a well-rounded position, jaw slightly dropped and no diphthong)		cosi [kozi]
	[ɔ]	open as in 'hot'		oggi [ɔdʒi]
U	[u]	as in 'food' or 'rude'		tu [tu]

(Please check the pronunciation guides carefully for open and closed vowels as Italian spelling does not differentiate these sounds.)

NB: There are no diphthongs in Italian – the vowels are often liaised but nevertheless, clearly delineated.

Semi-Vowels

[j]	as in 'yard'		piano [pjanɔ]
[w]	as in 'water'		acqua [ak:kwa]

Consonants

B, F, M and V are pronounced as in English
D, N, T and L are pronounced as in English but with the tip of the tongue in a forward position, just behind the upper front teeth.

C	[tʃ]	as in 'church'	*[before **e** or **i**]*	ciel [tʃel]
C	[k]	as in 'cook'		cantata [kantata]
SC	[ʃ]	as in 'shoe'	*[before **e** or **i**]*	scena [ʃena]
SC	[sk]	as in 'skull'		scala [skala], scherzo [skertsɔ]
G	[ʤ]	as in 'jar'	*[before **e** or **i**]*	giorni [ʤorni]
G	[g]	as in 'good'		largo [largɔ]
P	[p]	as in 'pull'		pace [patʃe]
QU	[kw]	as in 'quick'		quartetto [kwartet:tɔ]
R	[ɾ]	slightly flipped 'r'	*[between two vowels]*	caro [karɔ]
R	[r]	trilled/rolled 'r'		ritardando [ritardandɔ]
S	[s]	as in 'so'		subito [subitɔ]
S	[z]	as in 'zoo'		deciso [detʃizɔ]
Z	[ts]	as in 'pets'		grazia [grat:tsja]
Z	[dz]	as in 'adds'		mezzo [med:dzɔ]

Extra Notes

-GLI-	[ʎ]	like 'million'	*[the **g** is silent]*	scoglio [skoʎɔ]
-GN-	[ɲ]	like 'new' (ny-oo)	*[the **g** is silent]*	segno [senɔ]
H		is always silent		hanno [an:nɔ]
H		hardens C, G an SC		che [ke] scherzo [skertsɔ]
I		is silent when used to soften C, G, or SC		già [ʤa] lascia [laʃa]

Double consonants

Any double consonants should be emphasised with a slight 'stop' of the vowel before them – as in allegretto [al:legret:tɔ], cessa [tʃɛs:sa]. A single **r** is lightly flipped. A double **rr** is strongly rolled.

Word endings

When singing in Italian, final vowels (unless marked with an accent eg: più) should never be stressed.

Key to International Phonetic Alphabet for German

Vowels	IPA	English Sounds	German Words
A	[aː]	long – as in 'far'	Vater [faːtə]
	[a]	short – as in 'undo'	Mann [man]
E	[eː]	long – no direct English equivalent but exactly the same as French é (prepare your tongue as if to say 'ee' and say 'ay' without dropping the jaw)	jenem [jeːnəm]
	[ɛ]	short – as in 'bed' or 'set'	denn [dɛn]
	[ə]	neutral – as in 'the' or 'again'	deine [dainə]
I	[iː]	long – as in 'see' or 'police'`	die [diː], ihm [‖iːm]
	[ɪ]	short – as in 'sit' or 'bin'	im [‖ɪm], ich [‖ɪç]
O	[oː]	long (say 'oh' with lips almost as closed as if for 'ooh' and with no diphthong)	froh [froː]
	[ɔ]	short – as in 'hot'	kommt [kɔmt]
U	[uː]	long – as in 'food' or 'rude'	Blumen [bluːmən]
	[ʊ]	short – as in 'put' or 'book'	und [‖ʊnt], um [‖ʊm]

Modified Vowels

ä	[ɛː]	long – as in 'gate'	Mädchen [mɛːtçən]
	[ɛ]	short – as in 'bed' or German short 'e'	Hände [hɛndə]
ö	[œ]	short – the same sound as 'earth' but shorter	Hölle [hœlə]
	[øː]	long – as above but with lips more closed (the same as French 'deux'	schöne [ʃøːnə]
ü	[yː]	long (say 'ee' with closed lips in an 'oo' shape)	über [‖yːbɐ], Frühling [fryːlɪŋ]
	[ʏ]	short (try saying 'it' with closed lips in an 'oo' shape)	Müller [mʏlə]

Dipthongs

ai, ei	[ai]	as in 'aisle' or 'height'	Mai [mai], mein [main]
au	[au]	as in 'house' or 'flower'	Haus [haus], Frau [frau]
äu, eu	[ɔi]	as in 'boy' or 'oil'	bräutigam [brɔitɪgam], neu [nɔi]

As in English, when singing a diphthong, the singer must spend most time on the first of the combined vowels, leaving the second
to the last moment before finishing the word or syllable.

Glottal Stop [|]

The slight stopping of the breath and starting the sound (as in 'umbrella') takes place in German before any word beginning with a vowel. The intensity of this is open to artistic interpretation, but it should never be overdone or in danger of injuring the voice.

Consonants

Consonants are pronounced as in English with the following exceptions:

g is always pronounced hard as in 'good' (*but see* '**Endings**', page 79) Gold [gɔlt]
h is silent after a vowel, otherwise it is aspirated Sohn [zoːn], Hand [hant]
j is pronounced as an English 'y' as in 'yes' jung [jʊŋ]
k is pronounced before 'n' (it is never silent) Knabe [knaːbə]
r is slightly 'flipped' [ɾ] before a consonant sterben [ʃtɛrbən]
r is rolled [r] at the beginning of word or after another consonant Rose [roːzə], Grab [grap]
s before vowels, as in English 'z' (*but see below*) sein [zain], Rose [roːzə]
v mostly as in English 'f' Vater [faːtə]
w as in English 'v' Wenn [vɛn]
z as in 'cats' zum [tsʊm], Tanz [tants]

Double consonants and other sounds

ck	[k]	as in 'lock'	Glück [glyːk]
ch	[x]	after a, o, u and au – closest to Scottish 'loch' (place tongue in the position for 'k' and say 'h')	hoch [hox], nach [nax]
ch	[ç]	after e, i, ä, eu or a consonant as in (whispered) 'yes' (place tongue in the position for 'ee and say 'h')	ich [‖ɪç], nächste [nɛːçstə]

ph	[f]	as in 'telephone'	Phantasie [fantazi:]
pf	[pf]	both letters sounded	Pfeife [pfaifə]
qu	[kv]	sounds like English 'kv ...'	Qual [kva:l]
ß	[s]	as in 'ki__ss'	Kuß [kʊs]
sch	[ʃ]	as in English 'ship'	schöne [ʃø:nə]
sp, st	[ʃp, ʃt]	sounds like English 'sht' or 'shp' (*at the beginning of a word, or after a prefix*)	Spiel [ʃpi:l], still [ʃtɪl] erstanden [‖ɛɐʃtandən]
-ng	[ŋ]	as in 'sing'	kling [klɪŋ]

Note: Unlike Italian, where double consonants are marked, in German, they are treated as single consonants unless the need to express the word more imaginatively leads to emphasising them (and this would be equally true of single consonants also).

Endings of words/prefixes/word elements

-er	[ɐ]	as in 'sister'	vater [fatɐ]
-r	[ɐ]	usually not pronounced (but check IPA in songs for exceptions)	nur [nu:ɐ], vor [fo:ɐ]
-en	[ən]	as in 'garden'	denken [dɛnkən]
b		at the end of a word sounds 'p'	Lieb [li:p]
d		at the end of a word sounds 't'	Lied [li:t], Grund [grʊnt]
s		at the end of a word as in 'less'	kleines [klainəs]
g		at the end of a word sounds 'k'	Sonntag [zɔnta:k]
-ig	[ɪç]	as in the German word 'ich'	ewig [‖e:vɪç]

General note

Even though there are many consonants in German, the legato line (as in all singing) is still paramount and consonants need to be quick and crisp.

Key to International Phonetic Alphabet for French

Vowels	IPA	English Sounds	French Words
a	[ɑ]	long – as in 'far'	âme [ɑmə]
	[a]	short – as in a bright 'ah'	la [la], caché [kaʃe]
e	[e]	long (prepare your tongue as if to say 'ee' and say 'ay' without dropping the jaw)	été [ete], et [e]
	[ɛ]	short – as in 'bed' or 'set'	est [ɛ], belle [bɛlə]
	[ə]	neutral – as in 'the'	le [lə], que [kə]
i	[i]	long – as in 'see' or 'police'	si [si], qui [ki]
o	[o]	long (say 'oh' with lips in a well-rounded position, jaw slightly dropped and no diphthong)	rose [ʀozə], vos [vo]
	[ɔ]	short – as in 'hot'	comme [kɔmə], col [kɔl]
u	[y]	long (say 'ee' with well-rounded lips in an 'oo' shape)	tu [ty], une [ynə]
ou	[u]	long – as in 'food' or 'rude'	tous [tus], pour [puʀ]
eu	[œ]	open (say 'earth' and drop the jaw)	leur [lœʀ], coeur [kœʀ]
	[ø]	closed (as above but with lips well-rounded)	deux [dø], feu [fø]

Nasalized Vowels

	[ɑ̃]	long [ɑ] (far) nasalized	blanc [blɑ̃], semble [sɑ̃blə]
	[ɛ̃]	short [æ] (fat) nasalized	sein [sɛ̃], essaim [esɛ̃]
	[õ]	long [o] (oh) nasalized	mon [mõ], ombre [õbʀə]
	[œ̃]	short [œ] (earth) nasalized	un [œ̃], parfum [paʀfœ̃]

Although nasal vowels are always followed by an **-n** or **-m** in the spelling, these consonants are **not** pronounced either in speech or singing.

Semi Vowels

	[j]	using an English 'y' sound as in 'piano'	bien [bjɛ̃], pied [pje]
	[w]	as in 'quack'	moi [mwa], voyons [vwajõ]
	[ɥ]	Try to say the 'y' in 'une' very quickly before the 'i'. It should not sound like a 'w'.	puis [pɥi], luit [lɥi]

Consonants

b d f k l m n p t v w y x z

The above consonants are pronounced as in English though in French (as in Italian) there is no explosion of breath with **p, t, k**. Also double consonants are not marked and are spoken or sung as if single.

c	[k]	hard as in 'cook'	*before a,o,u/ending words*	comme [kɔmə], lac [lak]
c/ç	[s]	soft as in 'piece'	*c- before e, i/ç- before a, u, o*	cesse [sɛsə], français [fʀɑ̃sɛ]
g	[g]	hard as in 'good'	*before a, o, u*	gauche [goʃə]
	[ʒ]	soft as in 'pleasure'	*before e, i*	age [aʒə]
h		is usually silent		horreur [ɔʀœʀ]
j	[ʒ]	is pronounced as in 'pleasure'		je [ʒə], jeune [ʒœnə]
l	[l]	like an Italian 'forward' 'l' (soft and quick) – *but also sometimes silent*		lac [lak], gentil [ʒɑ̃ti]
qu	[k]	pronounced as a 'k' and without the 'w'		que [kə], qui [ki]
r	[ʀ]	uvula is vibrated by a vocalised breath against the back of the tongue (see note below)		briser [bʀize]
s	[s]	unvoiced as in 'so'		souffrir [sufʀiʀ]
	[z]	voiced as in 'gaze'	*between two vowels*	cousin [kuzɛ̃]
x	[ks]	as in 'example'		extreme [ɛkstʀɛmə]
	[gs]	as in 'eggs'		examiner [ɛgzamine]
	[z]		*in a liaison*	deux‿amis [døzami]
		silent as a final consonant	*no liaison*	deux [dø], yeux [jø]

Other Sounds

-ai	[e]	closed 'e' at the end of a word	saurai [soʀe]
-ais/-ait/-aient	[ɛ]	open 'e' at the end of a word (verb endings)	mais (mɛ), avaient [avɛ̃]
-au/-eau	[o]	long (say 'oh' with lips in a well-rounded position, jaw slightly dropped and no diphthong)	beau [bo]
ch	[ʃ]	as in 'shoe'	chanter [ʃɑ̃te]
-ail	[aj]	as in English 'eye' (with a pronounced 'y')	travail [tʀavaj]
-eil	[ɛj]	as in English 'eh' followed by 'y'	meilleur (mɛjœʀ)
-euil/oeil	[œj]	as in English 'err' followed by 'y'	feuille (fœj), oeil (œj)
-ouille	[uj]	as in English 'ooh' followed by 'y'	mouiller [muje]
-er/ez	[e]	as a word ending	monter (mɔ̃te), assez (ase)
-gn-	[ɲ]	as in 'onion'	ligne (liɲə)
ph	[f]	as in 'telephone'	séraphin (seʀafɛ̃)
th	[t]	pronounced as a 't'	théatre (teatʀə)

Word endings

A final -e, -es and the verb ending -ent are silent in speech, but in singing are often given a note. These are sung to the neutral [ə] vowel but should never be emphasised and phrased off tastefully wherever possible.

Liaisons

The decision whether or not to join the final consonant (or consonant plus [ə]) to a following word beginning with a vowel is always a thorny one and the academic rules are complex. Contemporary tastes are always evolving and liaisons are used increasingly less frequently. In this volume, the IPA liaisons will be shown in brackets and should be executed gently and without too much emphasis.

Rolling the 'r' in French

In classical singing, it has been considered good taste to pronounce the rolled 'r' in the Italian style (i.e. with the tip of the tongue in a forward position). Contemporary tastes, however, seem to be moving towards the traditional uvular 'r', even in classical song and opera. In this guide, we recommend the uvular 'r' [ʀ]. In the Baroque repertoire (*Bois épais*), a rolled Italian 'r' would be considered stylistic.